Between Sunlight

Emily Kaye

Between Sunlight

© Emily Kaye Roberts, 2021.

Cover design and internal illustrations were acquired
through licenses with Shutterstock.com and Canva.com.

Paperback ISBN: 9798459933109

www.emilykayewrites.com

For those who are healing.

Dusk

Silence is pulling at my hair.
Moonlight is pinching on my skin.
Shadows are whispering in my ear.
Night is taunting me again.

I wasn't taught
the table manners of love.

I wasn't taught
to take small bites of people
then let my gut settle.

I either spit people out
and leave the table
or I devour them whole.

My voice is like water,
the way it reshapes itself,
fills the cracks of conversation,
moulds its flow
around other people's tongues.

Just once,
I want my voice to be solid,
develop a shape, form an edge,
change itself into ice if it must,
but give me something I can bite on.

Why do these feelings,
which burn like
forest fires in my gut,
always reduce to
smoke on my lips?

I cannot sleep in this mind.
It is tangled with dirty sheets.
I toss and turn in memories.
All my thoughts smell like you.

Depression
is like driving a mind
with fog on its windshield.

You know there's a
turn-off to happiness
somewhere.

But you can barely see
a life ahead of you.

We wrap our pinkie fingers
around love
like a wishbone,
promising to give equally to it,
and yet when it breaks,
one always loses more.

Your love
emptied my kindness.

Your kisses
dug out
all my roses.

I have only
thorns
left in my tongue.

How do we become strangers
after a love like ours?

I have loved you for centuries.
I knew your face before birth.

Your name
was conceived in my throat.

My soul
was derived from your atoms.

You are a part of my blood,
my second heartbeat.

How do I rip you from me now?
Unlearn you from my flesh?

How does one shed a leg
and continue walking?

Anger lives in me –
real and persistent as a heartbeat.

Sometimes
I want to cut it out of me.

Sometimes
it is all that is keeping me alive.

The fire
may not remember
its damage,
but the ash
can never forget.

How terrifying it is to be numb.

To be nothing but a grey cloud,
drifting through life,
not caring if you clear or storm
or dissolve.

That is how I love.
Holding on too tight.

White knuckles
around my emotions.

Trust
that bears fingernails.

I leave scratch marks
in every heart I touch.

How are we so close

but so far from each other?

I am laying in your arms,

tasting your lungs,

warming your blood with my own,

and yet,

when I look into your eyes,

I see your heart,

standing an ocean away,

but can't find the right words

to swim my own towards it.

They told me
the way to a man's heart
is through his stomach,
but they never cared to tell me
the way to my own.

Which, ironically,
was climbing out of
a man's stomach.

I am jealous of your silence,
of what steals your mind away.
When you ignore me,
I imagine that you are sitting
in a dark corner of your skin,
using the light of my voice
to read old love letters,
and when you reply,
you are shoving those secrets
into a bottom drawer.

As if I don't know they're there.

You speak
a thousand knives into me
then blame me
for the blood on the floor.

I try to have a backbone with you,
but you always manage to fold it,
to arch my spine into a crossbow.

And so, my lungs fumble
with the feelings inside of me,
trying to load words onto my tongue.

But my voice, like two calloused fingers
wavering on the tension of a thought,
always slip before I can release them.

Some days I want to save the world.
Some days I want to swallow it.

It wasn't until
I faded to a shadow
that I noticed you
always
standing in my sunlight.

When I am just a drop of myself,
I become that shallow wave
that crawls back to the shore,
a lonely fingertip
pulling on the sand for one last kiss.

When I am just the salt of me,
I care only to rinse you with my skin;
embed the scent of my tongue
along the coast of your neck.

When I am just a sliver of an ocean,
I want to dissolve myself into your land,
even when the depths of me
are pulling me back by my feet.

When I am at my weakest,
I would split myself against
every tide in my blood
just to hold a grain of you.

My mind is a forest.

My thoughts are the trees.

Depression is the thing
crouching in the shadows,
waiting to sink its teeth in me.

They say poets just need
to write the pain out of them
but I fear if I do that
I mightn't have
a single sheet of paper
that isn't kerosene and ash.

The hands of men
have always
invaded my body.

From my teens,
their unwanted touch
has waged war on me,
turned my flesh
into a battlefield,
embedded mines
beneath my skin.

Now I don't know
where I can be touched
without exploding.

I feel that I do not belong.

I feel that I am a star
that rebelled
against the heavens
and imploded upon human life.

There is no reasoning
with depression.

I see the sun
and then when I don't see it
it's like it was never there.

You're always lingering
between the lines
of my writing
like a wolf –
biding your time,
licking your lips,
knowing eventually
you'll devour my every page.

Grief.
It grew on me, over time,
like a new layer of skin –
something necessary
to hold my mess together
and carry me through life –
only it gave me a different face.

I feel dust collecting in my bones.

I feel candles melting in my spirit.

I feel weeds growing over my dreams.

I feel myself slowly being withered by life.

Time doesn't heal.
It mocks.

Time stalks our pain,
steps on its heels,
bullies it to move along
quicker.

If anything,
Time keeps us
looking back
over our shoulder.

Sadness is a kind of drowning.

People let you go
because they fear you'll pull them in.

Sometimes I wish
my mind was a balloon,
something I could hold
outside of myself,
and, when it became too full,
I could simply untie it from my finger
and watch it float away.

Winter has moved in on our love –
the rivers of your voice
have frozen over,
every room in my mind
has a fireplace burning,
and when our hearts speak,
they speak in fog to each other.

Your smile looks like a bruise.
I kiss you like I'm dressing a wound.

My body feels jet-lagged
since you left me.

The clock in my chest
ticks three years behind
the rest of me.

My head and my soul
are in different time zones.

I wake in empty sheets,
and yet my heart still thinks
it's asleep in your arms.

If a man
forces his way
into your mouth
and tries to scrape out
sweet words from you,
if he wraps his fingers
around your tongue
and demands you drip
honey for him

give him bees.

Some memories live in me,
not as thought,
but as instinct.

An animal sense,
burning somewhere
between my blood
and my skin.

Humming
in the heat of my sweat.
Scraping
in the quiet of my skull.

No matter how much trauma
I undo from my mind,
like a clot in the vein,
a memory will come back to me.

As if it is imprinted in me,
buried somewhere
in the deep of my body,
not breathing but still alive.

I'm more of a writer than a talker.
Poetry lives in my flesh.

Cut me open
and you'll find tar-black
in my veins,
an inky pulse
beating with thoughts
unsaid.

My skin is like paper,
concealing words,
repeatedly
folding itself in halves.

Waiting for someone
to open me up and read me
without being compelled
to underline my heart in red ink.

My identity is always shifting.

Not decidedly pleasant
nor harsh –
I am what people create me.
A song ever-changing its keys.

The tune of my music
depends on the hands
pulling my strings.

It's too easy for people
to find their way out of me.

The footmarks of those who left
have worn a path
right through my heart.

Summer left with you that night.

I woke to find
the leaves of the willow tree
fallen like tears on the ground,
and the sun
tucked behind the clouds
as if it had curled itself
within a blanket.

It was as if autumn
and depression
had arrived overnight,
unbuttoned their coats,
and settled in for a long stay.

You stamp my love
into the ground
like a spark you cannot risk
getting out of control.

Lies flow from you

like bubbles of gum –

raspberry deceits

bursting

from your lips

in such soft, sugary promises –

I cannot help

but swallow them all.

I'm tired of
the fighting inside of me –
the insults that chase themselves
with knives around my head,
the tremor of doors
slamming in my heart,
the false promises
I make with myself afterwards –
that I will change,
that I will be kinder,
that I won't do it again.
But I do.

I'm tired of
the abusive relationship
I have with myself.

I want to leave.

My shoulders

are two desert dunes,

burning

for the moon of your head

to set upon them,

for the drought of your lips

to break upon this sand

and soothe

the lonely thirst in my flesh.

Don't mistake
the breadcrumbs of a new love
for a banquet
just because you starved
in your last.

My soul
was your ashtray.

Your favourite place
to put out pain.

In the evenings,
I like to hide away,
unzip my skin
and wear the shadows;
release the me
that hides
throughout the day.

I swear my ribs are made of elastic.
How do I hold
every feeling I've ever swallowed,
every insult I've ever chewed on,
every lie I've ever digested,
and not expel it all out of me?

I don't feel safe
with Love in the driver's seat.
It is too reckless with me.
It runs stop signs.
It ignores speed limits.
In love, my heart is
just an anxious passenger,
gripping its seatbelt,
waiting for the worst to happen.

I want to be happy
but it is like
all the butterflies
in my stomach
are trapped in spiderwebs.

Perhaps I don't need to
restitch myself
but rather
unravel completely
and begin again.

I am not your flower;
a delicate beauty
awaiting your pick,
an object to grasp
whenever you please,
a trophy to keep
on a sunless mantel
until I crisp.
I am here for myself.

Help me grow or leave me be.

I am like a toddler
the way I fight my body.

My skin
folds itself around me
and I pinch it.

My mind
kisses my cheek
and I bite it.

My pulse whispers
I love you,
and instead of saying
I love you too,
I hold my breath until
my heart falls unconscious.

I've consumed
poisonous relationships.
I've devoured thoughts
that have almost killed me.
Why then can't I swallow
a few spoonfuls of love
for the body
that has kept me alive?

I have grown apart from myself.

My mind no longer compliments me.

My soul no longer rubs my feet.

My heart and I sleep in different rooms.

Removing you
from my thoughts
is tearing salt
from the ocean.

I keep an eye on
the years in my past
like spot fires,
flickering
at the edge of my vision;

hazardous little memories
I have to be ready
to extinguish from my mind.

I cannot turn my back
on my thoughts for a second
and trust that they won't
burn me to the ground.

How does a heart break
across the world
and the whole planet
not feel its shudder?

I hear an injustice
beyond the sun
and rebellion burns
beneath my fingernails.

A tear drops
three countries away
and I feel the entire ocean
change its flow.

A soul aches
in a foreign wind
and I become thunder.

Your deepest wounds
need to be spoken.

Your life
will not taste sweet
while there is blood
in your mouth.

In love,
we are all just lost children
crying out in the darkness
for a warm pair of arms.

You can try to recreate someone –
to take their broken pieces,
the scraps of their love,
and, like Frankenstein,
try to build them into a better person
but, without a heart,
they will only ever be a monster.

I coast the waves
between company
and isolation,
never really sure
where to plant my feet.

You say *I love you*
not as if it flows from you
but as if you are
clearing something
from your throat –

as if my kisses leave
a bitter taste on your tongue,
or my feelings
are too thick to swallow.

You say *I love you*
as if my love is choking you,
and you say what you must
to expel me from your lungs.

I wish to be small today,
to curl myself in under my sheets –
how a pebble clings to a muddy bank –
and let life run, like a river, over me.

The world keeps trying
to pull beauty out of me
like a magic trick,
not realising I am the world,
and it is sawing itself in half.

My chest beats
in tiny earthquakes,
trembling for love,
aching to split itself open
and feel something.

Anxiety
feels like cold water
rising around my body,
a numbing dread
slowly
paralysing me in place.
I cannot move.
I cannot speak.
I can only wait
and gasp for air
as it fills every last space
of hope inside of me.

I am no longer myself.
Who I am has become
hidden inside of me.

When I behold my reflection,
I see a woman
peering out from two windows
that are my eyes,
distracted by a past in the distance.

And I am a stranger on her doorstep
with rocks in my fist,
wanting to shatter every pane of myself
just to get my own attention.

I fear that my dreams
will become fine china plates –
precious things
locked in a drawer for 'another day',
beautiful, empty pieces
that will never be eaten from.

I fear that I will wait so long
to use my talents
that I shall someday be dead,
and everyone will look inside me,
wipe dust away with their sleeve,
and ask *what was she waiting for?*

My soul,
precious thing
grasping my finger,
you are too small
for this world.

You think life
opens wide for you
but you don't see it
licks its teeth.

His mind
was a clenched fist.
I tried and tried
with my tender fingers
to pry it open,
but just as it would
unfold
softly in my palm,
he would close up again
and hit me with it.

We didn't mix, him and I,
like earth and water,
anything we built together
just sunk into mud.

The pain of my past
still clings to my insides
like ugly wallpaper –

long threads of curlicues
wrapped around me
like stitching on a wound.

And, no matter how much
I peel or scratch at it,
no matter how many layers
of happy I paint over myself,

at a certain angle
I can still catch a glimpse
of sadness
coming through my smile.

When the darkness buries you,
sometimes all you can do is
bud your hope, root your feet,
and try to bloom towards the light.

Dawn

Night is dissolving from my bones.

Clouds are parting deep within.

Sunlight is burning in my chest.

Dawn is rising beneath my skin.

I consider my lips
a budded rose –

they only open
when I have beauty to give.

You are a wild thing
in my thoughts.

A bloom that has
outgrown my mind,
and started sprouting
out of my eyes.

I feel you
throughout the day,
tangling your vines
around me.

I become a lazy thing,
picking at your petals,
clinging to sunlight.

Twirling in circles,
trying to catch glimpses
of the back of my head.

Intuition
was a stranger at my doorstep,
knocking on deaf ears.

Now she sits
in a warm corner of my mind
like a wise, old woman,
rocking in her chair.

And when she speaks,
I've learnt to pull up a cushion,
rest at her feet,
and listen.

I give my troubles
to the moon
and she breaks them
into stars.

Your ears
are two wishing wells
I whisper into
when you are sleeping.

At night,
I sit at your edge,
my feet
dangled into your depths,
and pour loving words,
my brightest gold,
into you.

In hope that
my wish for your heart
will come true.

I need more than the physical –

seduce thought from me,
undress my mind,
slip into my curiosity
until it screams with reason.

She was an artwork –
the unconventional sort,
the creation of a child
who couldn't keep within the lines.

An unapologetic, beautiful mess
that didn't need to be understood,
just loved for what it was.

Forcing inspiration is like
shouting for a bird
to rest on your shoulder.

Just picture a forest,
sit quietly in yourself
and it will come.

His eyes were whiskey –

two sweet drops
of golden brown
that livened me
with every sip.

Every gaze
was a hit of courage,
a zing of fire
burning through me.

Like any good drink,
he dizzied my soul
without stealing my mind.

Our friendship is telepathic.
It transcends distance.

Without needing to see you,
I know exactly what you're feeling,
what words sit in your throat.

As if we share a nervous system,
transmit thoughts through our hairs.

I could stand an ocean away
and still feel your pinkie finger
tugging on mine.

Savour your youth.

Scrounge up the hours
at the ends of your days
like loose change
and splurge on experiences
instead of responsibilities.
Leave love around you
like dirty laundry
you will worry about tomorrow.
Let the day wake you
like a lover's fingers in your hair,
and the night embrace you
like a midsummer campfire.
Search the world over,
turn it upside down,
rearrange it like couch cushions,
searching for the keys to yourself.

Live more and worry less
because youth is an adventure
from which there is no return.

Broken people are the most empathetic –
as if, through their jagged cracks,
they absorb the essence of the universe.

Artists do not create

for ego, or money, or fame.

They create because

there is a deep chattering inside

that needs to be silenced,

a world within asking

to be brought outside of itself.

They create to appease the person

that lives inside of them.

That second soul

that all artists are born with.

Because they are something not quite human.

I have made peace
with the scars on my skin.

I imagine that
every dent in me
is a fingerprint left
by God's healing hands.

Your hand found mine and,
in a heartbeat,
the world fell quiet –

the battling sea slowed to a waltz,
the winds reduced to whispers,
and the red sun, which had just
stretched its arms over the horizon,
held its breath.

In a heartbeat,
it was as if the world paused for a moment
just to marvel at us.

His eyes glowed
as if every star
in the universe
lived upon them.

That was how I knew
there was depth in him.

And in the silence that lingered
between our reading books,
and drinking tea, and painting art,
was the sweetest hum of mutual peace.

Every curve of my body

is a mountain

I will conquer with love.

Do not neglect yourself.
Your soul is worth knowing.
Pull off your shoes
and laze in its grasses.
Rinse your hair in its nectar.
Let its sunlight stain your skin.

Healing is painful.

It shifts everything inside.
It rearranges your bones.
It stretches your skin.
It unknots your spine.

Growing wings is painful.

There was a rare music
in his bloodstream
that my soul
wanted to dance to.

My soul dwells between worlds.

Half of me is always off.

One foot in the trees, the other in the seas.

I've never seen both sides of my face.

I want our love to be forever filled with play –
for our souls to always tease each other,
push back and forth like teenagers on swings.
I want to always hopscotch through your thoughts,
and for you to skip stones across my silence.
I want to spend mornings swimming in your eyes,
and evenings stretching the hours like taffy.
I want to grow old with you in a love that never ages.

Your love falls into me

like honey

dripping into tea;

soft drops of gold

sinking

right to the bottom of me.

I can feel your sweetness

spreading

through my blood.

There is such beauty in her soul
that when she walks in the ocean,
the waves rise up around her
like sinners in church —
reaching out their hands,
crashing upon their knees,
begging to be blessed by her holy skin.

Today I choose to love myself.

Today I greet my body
with a bouquet of flowers
on my tongue
and kiss
a dozen red apologies
into my skin.

Today I choose to forgive myself.

It is more than goosebumps.

Your love raises
tiny volcanoes in my skin.

When I am with you,
every atom of me burns.

When you touch me,
every beat of my chest
whispers *erupt me.*

My frown
is like a crooked frame
hanging from my face.

He cannot notice it in a room
and not straighten it
with the fingertip of his lips.

I want beliefs I can carry
like flowers in my hair —
little growths of beauty
I can pluck from my knots
and pass onto others.

I want to leave no harm
or heartache where I wander,
just a trail of love
scattered like petals,
by the handful.

I am the architect
of my person –
continuously building
and rebuilding myself.
Repairing walls
in my values.
Sealing holes
in my integrity.
I am always changing.
I am always new.

I cannot hate my body.
For it was this skin
I was wearing
when the sun learned my name.
This is who I was
when I first tasted the wind.
It was my hand
I was holding when I woke,
and it will be my hand
I'm holding when I pass.
I cannot hate my body
for I am because of it.

So different are the sea and the sky,

and yet they are inseparable from each other.

Like wild horses, they run at each other's sides,

closer than air, but never are they one and the same.

Even as they bend and dip into each other,

you can tell the two apart.

Never does one try to change itself into the other,

nor the other into itself.

They are always connected but always their own.

As if your heart were
a splintered thing
and my pen were pliers.
I wish to pluck you with words,
each stroke of ink
a delicate pull within,
until there is no place
that you are hurting.

His shirt was like a sundial –
the open buttons measuring
the hour of wine he was in.
I'd know the day had ended
when he would lay down beside me,
wearing nothing
but a crescent-moon grin.

I miss places I've never been to.

I feel pulled towards windows,
drawn by the scent of other lands,
mouth watering to cross the ocean.

I ache deeply beneath my skin.
A phantom pain for pieces of me
that do not exist,
but belong to me, nonetheless –

divided parts of my soul
that lie scattered across the planet,
waiting on me
to put them back together again.

I can hear my own voice on the wind,
beckoning me to my feet –
calling me to be lost,
calling me to be found.

I feel people deeply.

My skin is an open void,
continually absorbing
the atmosphere around me.

A lung with a face on,
I am but an organ
breathing people into me –

dissolving their fears, their joys,
into the lining of my heart.

I hold a connection with every life.

I share a pulse with the earth.

When you love a person,
it is not enough to know them.

You must climb inside of their skin
and walk around in it for a while.

You must peer into their mind
and learn where it is broken.

You must water their heart
and see if it grows.

You must learn how someone works
before you can know how to love them.

When I feel myself closing in,
he reminds me that a butterfly
has no use for a cocoon.

Do you see how Autumn sighs?
How she clicks
the years out of her shoulders
and rinses her hair in the wind?

Do you see how she changes herself?
How she dulls the colour of her eyes
and sheds her mind upon the ground?

Even nature
has to rest and recharge sometimes.
Even nature
has to take a deep breath
and exhale the past from its bones.

It's okay to let your heart fall off
for a few months
and softly sprout a new one.

I've shed
so many layers of myself,
so many personalities,
that now my inner child
stares back at me in the mirror –
a glint of hope in her eyes
that I will be the one.

The one to give her
all the love she ever needed.

I searched the world for peace
only to find it living inside of me –
tucked away in an attic
behind everyone else's junk.

.

Spring
found its way into me
and bloomed hope
from roots of misery.

I collect pain from my soul
like sage from the garden.
I dry it out, store it,
then I brew it into words —
an elixir of experiences
others can lick off my pages
to heal themselves.

Then, one day,
forgiveness rolled in
like a tide to the shore
and washed your footprints
from my mind.

No.
So soft, yet so powerful.
It holds weight.
It demands space.
It shifts planets.

No forms mountains
around the soul.
It drains oceans
from the gut.

No stretches the sky,
splits open the stars,
creates one a universe of their own.

Gold doesn't burn in the flames.

It flows.

I like how my name
sounds in your mouth,
how gently it flows
from your lips,
like a warm breath
against a dandelion.

A wish you call upon.

Like books,
I prefer people a little shabby –
with worn covers,
and fragile pages,
and dog-ears in their hearts.

I prefer the forgotten souls
on life's bottom shelf,
resisting perfection.

I relate to their stories the most.

Children.

They are something other-worldly.

Carriers of great wisdom,

young ancestors of the earth.

They hold centuries of stories in them.

They see in colours that we have forgotten.

They laugh in languages that are extinct.

They remember the other side of life,

the very blueprint of heaven.

They run with angel-dust on their shoulders.

Silence –
have you always had this voice?
Soft and open
as the vowels in his name?
Clean and bright
as the paper before the poem?
Vast and still
as the ocean after the storm?

Until now,
I had not heard you this way;
like warm caramel
seeping into the rose of my ear,
softly clogging my thoughts,
filling my head
with sugary nothingness.

I hear you now and I am empty,
I am full.

I believe they call it peace.

I'd study his face,
trace it with my fingers –
trying to memorise
every line
collected in his skin.
Every crease of pain,
every dimple of joy,
as if it were a map
that might lead me
to the deepest depths
of his truest self.

I have vigour in my bones,
an ache to write oceans,
a hunger for the blue in the sky.

I have lust in my fingertips,
hurricanes in my lungs,
a life inside me, waiting to fly.

Loving myself
wasn't some elegant affair –
a graceful transition
into self-acceptance,
a debutante
slipping into a silk dress.
There were no white gloves,
just bare fists
thrashing in the darkness
after the sirens woke me,
hot blood and tears and panic.
It was a matter of survival –
resistance against everyone
who ever made me feel like
I didn't deserve to be here.

So, if I glimmer with gold,
it's only because I won the war.

A misconception it is,
that beauty
diminishes with age.

Why, the stars have burned
for billions of years
and still paint
the most enchanting of skies.

Your heartbeat is a rebellion.
Every pound against your chest
is a fist on the door of the world,
reminding all within its walls that,
despite everything, you are still here.

You must stop tapping
on people's shoulders,
pulling on their hems,
moping about
like a hungry child
with its hand outstretched,
hoping someone
will give you your worth.

It is nobody else's.

I'm learning to give love
like the sun,
which doesn't elect
where it pours its light,
it just pours.

I'm learning that kindness
is a kind of oxygen
that must be breathed out
once it has filled us.

I'm learning that happiness
is a wavering feeling –
a flower in the hand,
which cannot be held forever,
but, for the moment it lasts,
a truly beautiful thing.

It was a moment
when she entered a room,
such an elegant beauty,
as if a toast
was being held for her,
her name would fizz
like champagne
on the lips of everyone
caught in her glow.

We have so few
breaths on this earth.

Don't miss an opportunity
to tell someone
they've taken yours away.

We slipped into love
with the ease of falling snow,
gently but suddenly,
with a tingling in every toe.

I am a different woman at 3am.
The walls start talking to me.
The planets in my head
revolve at twice the speed.
I become restless.

I want to wander upwards,
make snow angels in the stars.
I want to undress my skin
and lather the night on my bones.

I feel wild beneath the moonlight,
as if tides in my veins are being pulled
to the farthest corners of the earth.

The stone
that faces the sky
will believe it is a mountain.

How is it
that I am broken
but also beautiful to you?

How did you take my broken glass,
like soft petals in your hands,
and assemble them into a chandelier
at the entrance hall of your heart?

How is it that I am
the first thing people notice
when they set foot in you,
the first nameplate on your tongue?

How is it that I am
what you're gazing up at
when you tell people
this is my home?

I used to silence my feelings.

Now they speak before I do.

Therapy
is a necessary undressing,
a baring of the mind,
an opening wide for oneself.

Therapy
is bathing naked in the springs
of *whom we want to be,*
while letting
whom we didn't choose to be
be softly cleansed from our skin.

Every door I ever slammed
on my heart
echoed back to me
like a pulse.

Every full stop I ever wrote
on my soul
planted itself like a seed
and grew.

Every time I tried to leave
my body
it always fought for me
to stay.

I no longer feel
the hollowness
of those who left me.

Their empty spaces
are simply rooms
I intend to fill
with beautiful things.

Until you have searched
for yourself
and found peace

do not come looking for me.

Grow daisies in your eyes.

Write love letters to your mind.

Raise suns with your lips.

Wear hope like a spine.

Treat your heartbeat like a honeymoon.

Fill your pockets with love.

Hold your tongue out to life

as if no drop is enough.

If you think you are
alone in your sadness,
you need only to
listen to the rain,
to hear a million drops
collapsing at once,
to know that all who ache alone

do not.

You are the river
rushing down my spine.

You are the spring
opening my flowers.

You are the ocean
drowning my troubles.

You are the sun
warming my spirit.

You are the universe
thriving inside of me.

Forgiveness
unlatches that cage
in your chest,
releases the grudge
that is beating its wings
against your bones.
Forgiveness says to pain
you are free to fly from me.

Your love softens me,
unclenches my soul,
warms me so deeply
that, by your touch alone,
I feel my heart
break out in a sweat
and every pore of me
open.

There are miracles
still waking inside of you –
rubbing their eyes,
patting their cheeks,
rising for their moment.

Be patient.

I am unburying the women in me;
rinsing darkness from their bones,
poking flowers into their hearts,
braiding apologies into their hair.

I am recovering every person in me
that I left out in the dark –
building them shrines
in the softest gardens of my soul.

He holds my feet
between his hands
with such gratitude
that I imagine
he is praying upon them –
blessing them
for having walked
my whole life
to find him.

When I am around you,
I am not myself.

My mind shrinks to half its size,
and my tongue doubles itself.

My feet switch places on me,
and my heart forgets to breathe.

When I am around you,
I forget any language
that isn't dripping down my skin.

I imagined my healing
would be like flowers
sprouting out of dead earth.

Instead, it was the tender lesson
that beauty might not grow
in every part of me

but that doesn't mean
that every part of me
doesn't deserve to feel the sun.

You will emerge from this darkness
with the light of a new sun.
You are a survivor of the night.
You are a day that has just begun.

Acknowledgments

Wow. Where do I even begin? I can't believe I've written my first book and that you are here, reading it along with me – this is an absolute dream come true for me, so I would, first of all, like to thank **you**, the reader, for investing your time and energy into reading my debut book, 'Between Sunlight'. I appreciate it more than you know.

I would also like to thank all my family and friends for supporting me and, of course, J for his ongoing inspiration. As well, I would like to thank all the amazing writers and poets before me – who touched my heart and made me fall so deeply in love with words. I hope I never stop writing, and all these people I've acknowledged make that dream all the more possible.

So, again, thank you.

STAY CONNECTED WITH ME
@emilykayewrites
www.emilykayewrites.com
There is more to come.

Printed in Great Britain
by Amazon